OJAI

California's Shangri-La

Published by:
CHD Publishers
Post Office Box 995
Ojai, California 93024
805-646-0541

ISBN 0-9624313-0-3 Hard Cover
ISBN 0-9624313-1-1Soft Cover

Photography: Bruce Ditchfield
Art Direction: Bruce Ditchfield,
                            Heather McKenzie
Text: Glenn Emanuel/Bruce Ditchfield
Typography/Mechanicals: Rubén Acevedo
Printing: Dai Nippon Printing Co., Ltd.
Liaison: Kohei Tsumori

Cameras:
Nikon 35mm
Hasselblad 2 1/4
Sinar 4x5

Films:
Kodachrome 25, 64
Ektachrome 64

Ojai, California

Contents

Maricopa Mountains

I'm sure all of us have heard stories of how it "was" in our hometown. I had one of those experiences too.

An Ojai oldtimer told me how the river by Soule Park used to run year round and how Steelhead Trout used to spawn up to Senior Canyon. He told me how there were bear and mountain lion in downtown Ojai and condors flying overhead.

Those days are gone.

I remember 25 years ago I'd see deer, rabbits, and quail every morning in abundance. Where are they now? Does this say something about nature's delicate balance changing?
What species is next? When will it be our turn to live in a protected place away from our own hostility? Is there a message here?
A message from our planet, suffering from the weight of a thoughtless humanity?

Our species has grown and the Earth has not. God stopped making dirt long ago. We can't unconsciously or justifiably keep raping our world, our only home.

Some of the most desolate and smog choked places in the world today were once the finest.
When we become environmentally conscious the numbers multiply rapidly in all of our favors.

What we've done we can undo.
This book is a tribute to returning our Earth to a place of self-esteem.
It's time to let our prayers become our actions.

"The only place to start changing the world is by cleaning up your own hometown." -Jackson Browne

"If you told me 30 years ago that we'd have a hole in our sky I wouldn't have believed you. However if you told me 30 years ago the Berlin Wall would come down, I wouldn't have believed you either. We will clean-up these environmental problems." -Paul McCartney

Matilija Canyon

Dawn

Lake Casitas

View From
Senior Canyon

Leisure Hills

To the West...

Matilija Canyon
Maricopa
Casitas

Creek Road

Rancho Matilija

Piedra Blanca

Buckthorn and Lake Casitas

Saddle Mountain

Journey East...

East End
Upper Ojai

Ladera Canyon

East end
orange orchards

East End

Upper Ojai

Lower McNell Rd.

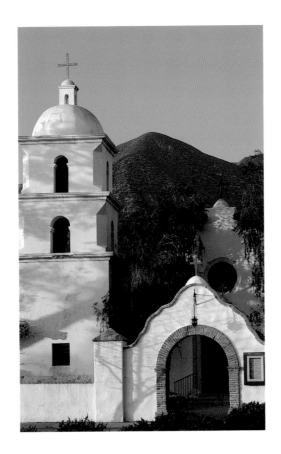

The Village

At every turning the myriad jeweled Ojai Valley sparkles. Fields of wildflowers fill one's vision to the brim. Welling mountains nestle and embrace the abundant fruitlands of the town and valley. The setting sun annoints the towering Topa-Topa bluffs with glowing translucent pink light. A mountain ridge sculpted by the forces of nature resembles an Indian chief lying in repose, contemplating the heavens. The wafting aroma of orange blossoms sweetens the air of a moonlit night. Caught in the spell of the shifting patterns of light, shadow and sky, mist and moonlight, one is transported to other times and places.

Participating in the splendor of California's southern coastal mountain range, Ojai rests in a pocket of mountains that form the backdrop for the seaside communities of Santa Barbara and Ventura. Inland twenty miles from the sea and laced with scenic roads, Ojai is a discovery of unusual proportion.

Greeted by graceful splendor, the entrances to Ojai (Chumash Indian for "nest") are majestic. From the mouth of Casitas Pass, named Koyos by the Chumash (meaning beginning), roars the Pacific Ocean. Salty and invigorating ocean air breathes inland along hillsides abundant with avocado and orange groves. Lake Casitas, site of the 1984 Olympic rowing events, lies below the road's many jutting ledges. Entering from the east, one is met by the pristine elegance of vast open fields, groves of apricot and walnut trees, and a stunning view of the entire Ojai Valley. Writer James Hilton, guided by Connie Wash to the top of Dennison Grade, ended his search for a site for the film Lost Horizon (1937).

Ojai as a community has responded to the beauty of its surroundings. A town of warmth, charm and depth, vigilant and thoughtful community effort has gone into preserving the natural simplicity and wealth of the land. Street and shop signs are made of wood; oak trees sit midstreet, protected by city ordinance. It has been said of this valley, "It has a charm others do not. . . In India, Greece and other civilizations, when they find a beautiful spot like this, they put up a temple. . .and the feeling you have is of a sacred place. . .be quiet, be gentle."

Beneath the surface of these thoughful values is a depth of undiscovered country: the essence of Ojai. With a history of spiritual purpose, its populace enjoy a lifestyle unique in outlook. A mecca for spiritual groups, Ojai received the attention of the Los Angeles Times as early as 1878: "The magnetic center for the earth is here. Spirit minded people come to reach the God centers in themselves." Meditation Mount, a lofty plateau with a phenomenal view of the valley, supports a world wide meditation group that disseminates its literature in eight different languages throughout the world.

The New Life Foundation founded by Vernon Howard, the philosopher and author of numerous inspirational books and Success Without Stress program, occupies eight scenic areas in the upper valley. The Krotona Institute of Theosophy, an international "brotherhood of humanity," settled in the valley in 1924 to establish a center for spiritual enlightenment emphasizing "the study of comparative religion, the investigation of the unexplained laws of nature, and the powers latent in man."

Discovered and reared by the Theosophists was the late Jiddu Krishnamurti. Declaring that "Truth is a pathless land," his observations of life and the workings of the mind rocked the foundations of spiritual and scientific thought. He went on to establish eight educational centers around the world, one in the Ojai Valley. Krishnamurti's public talks drew large numbers of people from around the world.

Annually since 1947, at the Libbey Bowl beneath oak trees and the warming May sky, musicians and music lovers take part in the Ojai Music Festival. Internationally acclaimed, this festival maintains an uncommon mixture of intimacy, exhilaration and tranquility.

Selections from little known classical treasures, avant-garde rarities, and musical morsels have made this gathering a rich musical feast. Frequently, composers oversee or conduct their work. Past musical directors include: Igor Stravinsky, Aaron Copland, Andre Previn, William Steinberg, Michael Tilson Thomas, Lukas Foss, Robert Craft, Pierre Boulez and Kent Nagano, Groups such as the L.A. Philharmonic, The Julliard String Quartet, The Boston Symphony Chamber Players, and special appearances by Ravi Shankar, The Kronos Quartet, and The Tokyo Quartet.

The music does not stop there. Folk dance, jazz, pop concerts, blues festivals, country fairs, an annual wine festival, film festivals, craft festivals, Shakespearean theater and lively children's theater have all become a part of Ojai's cultural scenery.

Besides artistic events, the works of local artists are deeply woven into the fabric of Ojai life. Exquisite galleries, fine pottery studios, and the artists themselves are among the many points of interest in Ojai's artistic community. One of the more renowned artists is the controversial potter, Beatrice Wood. Her whimsical creations and fanciful glazes have landed her work in The Smithsonian Institution, The San Francisco Museum of Art, and various other galleries throughout the world. Having concluded her autobiography in 1986 at the age of 93, she shows little sign of letting up on the spinning of pottery wheels or the spinning of interesting tales.

Hundreds of years ago the Spaniards chased Chief Matilija's party up what was to become Matilija Canyon. At a fork he sent his wife up a different canyon. The Spanish chased him up a neighboring canyon to where he jumped to his death. His wife later found his body and buried him. On his grave where she shed her tears, the first Matilija Poppy grew.

Laced with curiosities and distinctions, the story of Ojai remains rich and diversified for a community of its size. Edmund Libbey, was enthralled with Ojai and donated to the community the downtown arcade structure (1917) and the Ojai Valley Inn which gained recognition as "a structure in perfect harmony with its surroundings." Private schools abound throughout the valley. Aldous Huxley founded one and Howard Hughes is listed as alumnus of another. Albert Einstein and Thornton Wilder were guest summer school teachers and the Kennedy boys spent summers here at the same school. The nation's longest running Tennis Tournament has its roots here, begun in 1895 and hosting the talents of Billie Jean King, Jimmy Connors, and other great American champions. Jack Dempsey (World Heavyweight Boxing Champion 1919-1926) rested, trained and entertained with his boxing skills in Ojai between bouts. George Biggers was noted in Ripley's Believe It or Not for wearing a beard of live bees. Tara, the world's only roller skating elephant grew up and learned to skate in Ojai.

^ OAK GRILLE & TERRACE
THE CLUB
VISTA FINE DINING
THE NEFF LOUNGE

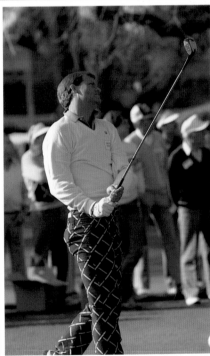

William Cook Baker (a name he promised himself if he won the government sponsored contest for creating the best tasting wheatless bread) produced numerous monumental cakes for various U.S. Presidents and a 1,000 lb. cake for the 1939 San Francisco World Fair. The world's smallest post office had a home at Wheeler's Hot Springs. The late John Lennon took secret residence in Ojai when the government refused to renew his visa. The population of 7,500 has only doubled since 1959 and supports over thirty five different religious groups.

Perhaps there are rare essences that echo from the hillsides, dance in the sunsets and permeate the currents of everyday life in the valley.

The Seasons

Shangri-La Views

View from Shelf Rd.

View from Krotona

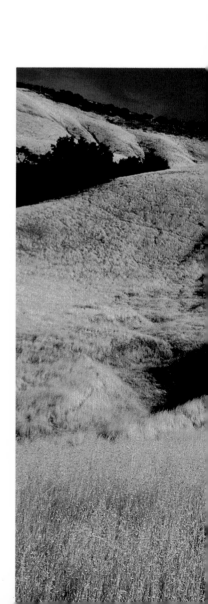

Soule Park

Boccali's Pumpkins

Moments

Zen

Casitas Ceanothus

Taft Hills

Black Mountain

Krotona Library

Casitas from Parker Hill

Dusk

This book is dedicated to my dad,
"Ditch" and Skyler.

Bruce Ditchfield